Susan B. Anthony

by Meish Goldish
illustrated by Brock Nicol

Harcourt

Orlando   Boston   Dallas   Chicago   San Diego

Visit *The Learning Site!*

www.harcourtschool.com

Today, women in the United States have the same voting rights as men. American men and women tend to take those rights for granted, but for a long time, they did not exist. Women gained equal rights as voters less than a hundred years ago.

American women owe thanks to many leaders who fought for suffrage for women—the right of women to vote. One person to whom they are indebted is Susan B. Anthony. She was one of the first Americans to speak out in favor of women's rights. It is largely because of her work and determination that women can now vote in all elections.

In the 1600s and 1700s, before Anthony's time, the only Americans allowed to vote were white men who owned property. It was thought that they made the best decisions since they had the most interest in good government.

In the American colonies, most women were not allowed to vote. Only a few colonies permitted widows who owned property to vote.

By the 1750s, however, many distinguished leaders were arguing that all colonists should have a say in their government. Because of this, the laws slowly changed. By 1820, nearly all white men could vote, even those without property. However, women still could not vote.

This situation is hard for us to believe today. Yet that is how things were when Susan B. Anthony was born in 1820. Her family members were Quakers. They believed that the law should guarantee equal rights for both men and women. They were also against the practice of slavery. Susan learned those values at an early age, and she took them very seriously.

At the age of nineteen, Susan B. Anthony became a schoolteacher. For ten years, she taught her students the importance of justice and equality. After a while, though, she wanted a wider audience. She tried to speak at rallies but quickly discovered that only men were allowed to talk there.

In 1851, she got a lucky break. She met Elizabeth Cady Stanton, another fighter for women's rights. The two women quickly became close friends and agreed to work together.

Stanton had already written a paper calling for women's equal rights. It was based on the Declaration of Independence. Stanton became an interpreter of the Declaration and wrote her own version of it to include rights for women.

For example, the Declaration states, "All men are created equal." Believing those words to be misleading and unfair, Stanton wrote in her own document, "All men *and women* are created equal."

Susan B. Anthony was influenced by Stanton. Soon, Anthony was working on women's rights in all possible ways. She even helped change the way women were allowed to dress.

At the time, women were expected to wear

long skirts. Instead, Anthony began to wear a type of baggy pants called bloomers. In 1851, most men were shocked to see women wearing such an outfit. Many thought that women should not wear pants because they looked silly. Thanks to Anthony, bloomers became a symbol for women's rights.

When the Civil War began in 1861, Anthony joined Stanton in the fight against slavery. Both knew "The Star Spangled Banner," a popular song that became our national anthem.

Anthony was bothered by the song's phrase, *the land of the free*. She felt that it was a lie. How could America be a free land as long as slaves weren't allowed to be free?

For that reason, Anthony supported the movement to outlaw slavery. She felt strongly that the government should provide equality for African Americans, as well as for women.

O'er the land
of the free
and the home
of the brave.

After the war ended in 1865, Anthony and Stanton broke away from the antislavery fighters. The two women were disappointed because the others showed little or no interest in suffrage for women. Many people supported the Fifteenth Amendment to the Constitution. It gave the vote to African American men but not to women.

To improve the situation, Anthony and Stanton formed the National Woman Suffrage Association. Their goal was to introduce a Constitutional amendment that would guarantee voting rights for women.

Between 1868 and 1870, Anthony published a weekly magazine called *The Revolution*. It was full of articles calling for women's rights. The magazine helped Anthony gain the support of more women, as well as more men.

Finally, Anthony and a group of women took an action that won them national attention. In 1872 in Rochester, New York, the women went to the polls and voted in the presidential election. Anthony knew that she would get into trouble for this action, but she wanted everyone to realize that it was unfair to prevent women from voting. Because Anthony had broken the law by voting, she was arrested and forced to stand trial.

The trial received national coverage, which Anthony had probably hoped for. During the trial, she gave an emotional speech defending her illegal act. Understanding why someone breaks the law stumps many people. However, Anthony argued that acting against an unfair law was really a brave and admirable deed.

Anthony was fined $100 for voting illegally. However, when she refused to pay the fine, no further actions were taken against her. An interpreter of the case might conclude that sympathy, if not the law, was on her side.

After the trial, Anthony continued to work for women's rights. She and Elizabeth Cady Stanton edited a book called *History of Woman Suffrage*. In 1892, Anthony became president of the National American Woman Suffrage Association. She served as its head for eight years.

Sadly, Anthony lost her lifelong friend, Elizabeth Cady Stanton, in 1902. Yet Stanton's tragic death did not keep Anthony from continuing her own work for women's rights. At age eighty-four, she formed a new suffrage organization with another distinguished female leader, Carrie Chapman Catt.

Susan B. Anthony continued her struggle for suffrage until her own death in 1906. Unfortunately, she did not live to see the Constitutional amendment that would guarantee a woman's right to vote.

Anthony, however, left behind a strong following. From 1910 to 1920, Carrie Chapman Catt and other supporters carried on the battle for women's equality. They led marches and other forms of protest in Washington, D.C., and elsewhere. Some women even chained themselves to the fence in front of the White House. Protesters were arrested and often sent to jail, where they went on strikes.

Finally, in 1920, fourteen years after Anthony's death, the Nineteenth Amendment to the Constitution was adopted. It guarantees the right of all U.S. citizens, both men and women, to vote.

All Americans are indebted to Susan B. Anthony for her achievements. Thanks to her work for equal rights, the phrase *the land of the free* in our national anthem is more meaningful than ever.

In 1979, the U.S. government issued a one-dollar coin with Susan B. Anthony's picture on it. She was the first woman ever to be honored on a U.S. coin in general circulation.